SCIENTISTS AND THEIR DISCOVERIES
LOUIS PASTEUR

SCIENTISTS AND THEIR DISCOVERIES

SCIENTISTS AND THEIR DISCOVERIES
LOUIS PASTEUR

HARVEY WARREN

MASON CREST

Mason Crest
450 Parkway Drive, Suite D
Broomall, Pennsylvania 19008
(866) MCP-BOOK (toll-free)
www.masoncrest.com

Printed and bound in the United States of America.

CPSIA Compliance Information: Batch #SD2018.
For further information, contact Mason Crest at 1-866-MCP-Book.

First printing
9 8 7 6 5 4 3 2 1

Library of Congress Cataloging-in-Publication Data

ISBN: 978-1-4222-4033-5 (hc)
ISBN: 978-1-4222-7765-2 (ebook)

Scientists and their Discoveries series ISBN: 978-1-4222-4023-6

Developed and Produced by National Highlights Inc.
Interior and cover design: Yolanda Van Cooten
Production: Michelle Luke

CONTENTS

KEY ICONS TO LOOK FOR:

 Words to understand: These words with their easy-to-understand definitions will increase the reader's understanding of the text while building vocabulary skills.

 Sidebars: This boxed material within the main text allows readers to build knowledge, gain insights, explore possibilities, and broaden their perspectives by weaving together additional information to provide realistic and holistic perspectives.

 Educational videos: Readers can view videos by scanning our QR codes, providing them with additional educational content to supplement the text. Examples include news coverage, moments in history, speeches, iconic sports moments, and much more!

 Text-dependent questions: These questions send the reader back to the text for more careful attention to the evidence presented there.

 Research projects: Readers are pointed toward areas of further inquiry connected to each chapter. Suggestions are provided for projects that encourage deeper research and analysis.

 Series glossary of key terms: This back-of-the-book glossary contains terminology used throughout the series. Words found here increase the reader's ability to read and comprehend higher-level books and articles in this field.

The French microbiologist Louis Pasteur showed that tiny organisms carried diseases and could spread them from one infected person or animal to another. His germ theory of disease is one of the most important ideas in medicine and other life sciences.

WORDS TO UNDERSTAND

dimorphic—a substance that exists in two different structural forms.

Ecole Normale—a school in Paris where teachers were trained.

polarized light—light that has been altered by being passed through a crystal or solution, so that its rays all travel in the same plane.

tartaric acid—an organic acid found in wine and other substances.

CHAPTER 1

A Great Disease Fighter

There are few men and women in history who are universally acknowledged to have been truly and completely great. There must have been flaws in their character somewhere, but they are hidden by the immense good produced by their life and work. These people are noted not only for their tremendous achievements, but also for their beauty of character. Leonardo da Vinci was such a person. Louis Pasteur was another.

In these cynical days, we are apt to regard with suspicion any claim to perfection. But this can be taken too far. It is rightly a source of inspiration to ordinary people like ourselves that such great men and women have existed, and their examples can help us in our daily lives. In the case of Leonardo, all who knew him testified to his delightful and generous character. Similarly with Louis Pasteur.

Pasteur lived in a terrible age in France—an age of revolution and civil war, of grinding poverty, of needless slaughter. It was an age of corruption at every social level, of cowardice, deceit and faithlessness. It was the age when two of the greatest French novelists, Honoré de Balzac and Émile Zola, exposed the lust and greed of their society. It was certainly not an age that was likely to encourage or even recognize human perfection without a sneering suggestion that an appearance of goodness was merely a façade.

Nevertheless it is most remarkable that no one has ever suggested that Pasteur was anything but a person of the utmost honor, integrity, and kindness, as well as having been intellectually one of the greatest scientists who ever lived.

Early Life and Education

Jean Joseph Pasteur, the father of Louis, was born in Besançon, France, in 1791. He became a tanner, like his father and grandfather before him. He was conscripted into the army in the Peninsular War of 1811. After the war, he returned peaceably to his work at Besançon. He was then a reserved man, careful and slow in his dealings with people. He fell in love with a young girl, whose character, in contrast, was active, enthusiastic, and full of imagination. The couple married in 1815, and migrated to Dôle, France.

Their first child lived for only a few months. In 1818 they had a daughter, and four years later, on Friday, December 27, 1822, Louis Pasteur was born. Two more daughters followed.

For family reasons Jean Joseph Pasteur had to leave Dôle to live in Marnoz, France, where he again set up as a tanner. However, the family did not stay

A plaque outside this house on the Rue des Tanners ("Street of the Tanners") in Dôle marks it as the birthplace of Louis Pasteur. The genius of science was born here on December 27, 1822.

This illustration of Pasteur's house shows what the Rue des Tanners looked like in the nineteenth century.

there very long. There was a tannery to let in the nearby town of Arbois, with a little house and a yard with pits for the preparation of the skins. Here the Pasteurs settled.

Young Louis went to the local schools. He was then a small boy, and became a good average pupil. He won several prizes, but was not especially outstanding. During his holidays he would go on fishing parties with his friends. He was also very good at drawing, and produced some pastels that were so good that his friends nicknamed him "the Artist."

Perhaps the first person to realize the divine spark in Louis was the headmaster of his school, Monsieur Romanet. He often used to take the young Louis for strolls around the school playground, talking to him about what he might do in the future.

When he was sixteen, the time came to discuss Louis's further education. A friend of his father, Captain Barbier, kindly offered to look after Louis if he went to school in Paris. Jean Joseph Pasteur hesitated, but eventually agreed that Louis should go. His close school friend, Jules Vercel, was also going. However, the expedition was not a success. Louis grew very homesick, and after only a few weeks, his father came to Paris to take him home.

Back in Arbois, Louis again took up drawing in pastels, and produced a little portrait gallery of the friends of the family.

The problem of his higher education remained. Pasteur decided to go to the Royal College at Besançon, 25 miles (40 kilometers) from his home. While he was there, he was able to see his family often and he did very well. He finished a degree of Bachelor of Letters in August 1840. At the end of the summer break,

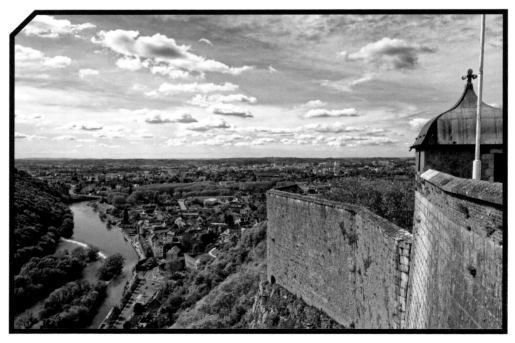

Aerial view of the old city and citadel of Besançon, a town in eastern France near the border with Switzerland. Pasteur attended the college there, earning a degree in 1840.

the headmaster of the Royal College of Besançon offered him the post of preparation master. He started this job in January 1841.

Louis Pasteur was now a serious and mature young man. It soon became clear that in time he would have to go back to Paris for his further education. Obviously, there were greater opportunities in the capital, and life was cheaper for a student there. In August 1842 Pasteur passed the examinations that allowed him to apply for admission to the **Ecole Normale**.

In October he set off with a friend. Once in Paris, he entered the Barbet boarding school, where he was a part-time teacher as well as a student. He attended classes at the Lycée St. Louis, and also went regularly to the Sorbonne to hear the lectures of Professor Jean-Baptiste Dumas, the renowned chemist. Dumas was one of the few teachers able to inspire enthusiasm as well as impart knowledge, and had an enormous influence on Pasteur.

Jean-Baptiste Dumas (1800–84) was an influential French chemist.

Pasteur settled down well to this new life, working hard and happily. He made himself so useful that he was soon able to pay his own way. At the end of the school year 1843, the results of his examinations were brilliant: several distinctions and a first prize in physics.

Pasteur was fourth on the list of those admitted to the Ecole Normale, where he started work with enthusiasm. During his holiday breaks he arranged to give lessons on physical science at Barbet's school.

Louis had grown into a grave, quiet, rather shy young man, tall and thoughtful, but full of dash and fire under this reserved façade. He read widely and his letters to his family show that he was very happy at this time.

Crystals and Light Rays

Pasteur was in the habit of taking long walks in the Luxembourg Gardens with his companion, Chappuis. On these walks they discussed everything—philosophy, history, and science. One day Pasteur began to talk about **tartaric acid**, which had been discovered in 1770 by the Swedish chemist Carl Wilhelm Scheele. When **polarized light** is passed through solutions of tartaric acid, the solution can turn the plane of the light to the right. So can solutions of ordinary sugar and crystals of certain quartzes. Some other substances, such as turpentine or quinine, rotate polarized light to the left. A rather mysterious substance called "racemic acid" had been studied by Joseph Louis Gay-Lussac and Jacob Berzelius. Chemically it looked similar to tartaric acid, but it did not rotate

For a short explanation of the effect of polarized light on racemic mixtures, scan here:

Models of crystals prepared by Pasteur in his work on the relationship between crystalline form, chemical composition, and the direction of rotatory polarization.

the plane of polarized light at all. Pasteur wanted to find out more about this substance. No one knew why it differed from tartaric acid in failing to polarize the light passed through it. This is typical of the kind of problem that Pasteur studied during the next few years.

Another problem Pasteur was interested in was **dimorphism**. Some substances produce different kinds of crystals if different methods of preparation are used. For example, sulfur melted in a crucible produces crystals that are quite unlike those obtained from solutions of sulfur in carbon disulphide. Such substances are called "dimorphic," and Pasteur studied the reasons why the different forms occur.

During the revolutionary year of 1848, Pasteur found himself in Paris. He joined the National Guard, and in an outburst of enthusiasm, gave all his savings to the cause of the Republic.

Meanwhile he continued his work as a teacher and on his research in chemistry. His absorption in the problem of tartaric acid soon bore fruit. He discovered that racemic acid was made up of two kinds of crystals, which differed in only one respect: some rotated the plane of polarized light to the right and others to the left. They were of a similar asymmetrical shape, and in fact were mirror images of one another. Pasteur had the idea that racemic acid did not rotate the plane of light at all because it was a mixture of equal quantities of these two types of acid. The two kinds of rotation canceled one another out.

The importance of this discovery was that it showed that similar organic chemicals could exist in two forms that differed only in that their crystals were mirror images and rotated light in different directions. We know now that the polarization happens not only in crystals but also in solutions of the substances. The actual molecules of the two forms are mirror images of one another in three dimensions.

As a result of his brilliant work, Pasteur was made Professor of Physics at the Lycée in Dijon. He arrived there in November 1848. However, he did not stay long, for in January he was appointed Professor of Chemistry at Strasbourg.

The new rector of the Academy of Strasbourg was named Laurent. He was an amiable and warm-hearted man. He and his wife and their two unmarried daughters welcomed Pasteur as a frequent guest to their home.

Only two weeks after Pasteur arrived in Strasbourg, he made up his mind to marry the second daughter. His proposal was accepted, and the young couple was married on May 29, 1849.

TEXT-DEPENDENT QUESTIONS

1. What was Jean Joseph Pasteur's occupation?
2. What college did Louis Pasteur graduate from in August 1840?
3. What did Pasteur discover about racemic acid?

RESEARCH PROJECT

Take a small piece of live weed from a pond; break off a leaf and place it on a dry, clean slide. On a microscope's high-power (400x) setting, you should see a pattern of rectangular cells. Adjust the diaphragm to the highest setting, which will allow the most light in, and after about a minute you should see green globs rotating around the outer edge of the cell. These are the chloroplasts, which gather light for the cell. When you expose them to light, they become excited and move rapidly.

Portrait of Marie Laurent Pasteur, taken in 1899. Madame Pasteur (1826–1910) was a very supportive wife, and often assisted her famous husband in his scientific work.

 WORDS TO UNDERSTAND

fermentation—chemical change of sugar to alcohol by yeasts and other similar kinds of chemical change by living organisms.

microbe—a living organism so small that it cannot be seen with the naked eye.

spontaneous generation—the theory that living organisms can originate from non-living matter.

CHAPTER 2

The Young Married Professor

Pasteur's marriage was ideal, largely because Madame Pasteur accepted from the first that the laboratory should come before anything else. She shared Louis's enthusiasms, hopes, anxieties, and joys, and provided him with the stable and happy home life that would serve as an essential background for his work.

Pasteur's future life was to be intensely active and busy. For such a life, a tranquil and stable private background is one of the greatest blessings, whose importance to its fortunate possessors cannot be overestimated. The achievements of great men and their effectiveness in life result from their temperament, moods, and self-confidence, as well as from their abilities. These personal qualities must obviously be affected by the intimate personal circumstances of their lives, of which the most far-reaching and all-pervading is their home background.

Pasteur's study of different varieties of tartaric acid and similar compounds took him on many trips into the old German Empire—Saxony, Trieste, Vienna, Leipzig, Freiberg, and Prague. In June 1853, in a telegram to his father, Louis announced that he had transformed tartaric acid into racemic acid artificially in the laboratory. There were now four different tartaric acids:

1. Dextro-tartaric acid, which rotates light to the right;

2. laevo-tartaric acid, which rotates light to the left;

3. the mixture of the two, which was optically inactive; and

4. mesotartaric acid, which was also optically inactive, but could not be separated into two components.

This differentiation into four types was a great advance, and for making it Pasteur was awarded the Red Ribbon of the Legion of Honour.

In Strasbourg, Pasteur moved his young and growing family into a larger house with a garden. Meanwhile, he went on studying the properties of crystals.

One of his observations was as follows. He broke an octahedral crystal and replaced one of the broken fragments in its mother liquor. It started to get bigger,

THE LEGION OF HONOUR

The Legion of Honour is the highest award given by the French government. It is an award given to both civilians and soldiers to recognize their achievements. Louis Pasteur was awarded the Legion of Honour in 1853 for his scientific discoveries. Recipients of the Legion of Honor wear a medal with a red ribbon.

The Legion of Honour was created in 1802 by Napoleon Bonaparte. Pasteur's father Jean Joseph Pasteur had received the award from Napoleon himself while serving in the French Army in 1814.

The National Order of the Legion of Honour is an organization of all those who were awarded the Legion of Honour. Its motto is "Honor and Fatherland." Members of the order meet in a building on the Left Bank of the Seine River, in a building known as the Palace of the Legion of Honour. The order is divided into five ranks: chevalier (knight), officer, commander, grand officer, and grand cross.

and after a few hours the broken end had resumed its original shape. Pasteur saw a similarity between this strange phenomenon and the healing of wounds, in which damaged living tissues resume their original form after a time. The great physiologist Claude Bernard was very impressed by this observation of likenesses between two such different happenings. Such recognition of similarities hidden under facts that apparently are far apart, Bernard felt, is one of the hallmarks of genius.

Other unexpected similarities between apparently unrelated phenomena stimulated Pasteur to think deeply about objects that were asymmetrical. He came to see "dissymmetry," as he called it, everywhere. "The universe is a dissymmetrical whole," was one of his sayings at the time. Another was "Life is dominated by dissymmetrical actions." Meanwhile Pasteur's work continued with the usual ups and downs experienced by any research scientist.

Physiologist Claude Bernard (1813–78) was a leading proponent of the scientific method. Bernard was a mentor and inspiration to Pasteur.

In September 1854, Pasteur was made a professor and the dean of the new Faculté des Sciences at Lille. This was a big chance for the young scientist, especially as there were many local distilleries where yeast **fermentations** could be studied.

Pasteur took a broad view of his duties as teacher and dean. It was an exciting time for the scientist. The electric telegraph had been invented; this and the other discoveries of modern science resulted in a great growth of industrial technology, that could easily be studied in the neighborhood of Lille. Pasteur took his pupils around factories and foundries and steel and metal works in the industrial areas of France and neighboring Belgium. He felt it was of great importance to show them the relationship between the different aspects of applied science.

His approach was optimistic yet practical. He felt that people should work hard to benefit humanity, and should think broadly. "In the field of observation, chance favors only the prepared mind" is a quotation from a speech he made at this time.

In 1857 Pasteur was a candidate for election to the Academy of Sciences. However, he failed to secure the necessary thirty votes. On his return to Lille, he set to work on the study of the fermentation of sour milk and showed that it was due to a yeast like the one that fermented beer.

The Ecole Normale in Paris was going through a difficult time, and Pasteur felt that he should go back there. He was appointed to take charge of the administration and direction of scientific studies. The scientific facilities were very poor. However, he cheerfully set out to study alcoholic fermentation. He found that glycerin and succinic acid were unexpected by-products of this process— where did they come from? He turned these problems over in his mind, too cautious to propound theories until the established facts justified them.

This period was marred by the death, in September 1859, of his eldest daughter, from typhoid fever.

Microbes and Spontaneous Generation

On January 30, 1860, the Academy of Science awarded Pasteur the prize for experimental physiology. It was his friend, Claude Bernard, who drew up the report on which this award was based.

Drawing of Pasteur around the time he returned to the Ecole Normale in Paris. A pin indicating his membership in the Order of the Legion of Honour is visible on his lapel.

Some of Pasteur's experimental apparatus on display at the Pasteur Institute in Paris.

Pasteur now started work on the problem of **spontaneous generation** of **microbes**. Since the days of Aristotle and Lucretius, many people had believed that microscopic animals could arise spontaneously out of non-living dirt and dust, and the philosophical revival in the middle of the eighteenth century again raised this problem in scientific circles.

Pasteur's aged teacher Biot had long felt that spontaneous generation did not occur, but had not managed to prove it. He tried to discourage Pasteur from going ahead, thinking that Pasteur would not get anywhere, but would waste a lot of time and energy.

In 1858, French naturalist Félix Archimède Pouchet, director of the Natural History Museum at Rouen, sent to the Academy of Sciences a paper strongly in favor of spontaneous generation. He proclaimed: "Animals and plants could be generated in a medium absolutely free from atmospheric air, and in which, therefore no germ of organic bodies could have been brought by air." Pasteur thought that Pouchet's work was not conclusive and wrote to him, "In experimental science it is always a mistake not to doubt when facts do not compel affirmation—in my opinion the question is not decisively proved. What is there in the air that gives rise to these creatures? Are they germs? Is it a solid? Is it a gas? Is it a fluid? Is it a principle such as ozone? All this is unknown and we

Scan here for a short video on Pasteur's spontaneous generation experiments:

French naturalist Félix-Archimède Pouchet (1800–72) was an opponent of Louis Pasteur's germ theory. He believed life could be spontaneously generated from non-living materials.

have to experiment to find the answers."

Pasteur plunged with enthusiasm into experimental work. He took a number of 250 cubic centimeter flasks and filled them with a suspension of yeast in water. He then boiled each flask and, while the fluid was still boiling, he closed the pointed opening through which the steam was escaping.

Pasteur divided these flasks into two groups. He broke the necks of one group, so that the surrounding air rushed in, bringing with it dust and yeast spores from the atmosphere. He then closed the necks again. The other group he left intact. Yeasts and mold grew in the flasks whose necks had been opened and that had thus been contaminated by the surrounding air. Nothing grew in the flasks that had been left sealed. This experiment showed that the development of microbes was not spontaneous, but had obviously been due to contamination. Pasteur backed it up with similar observations, all of which helped to demolish the theory of spontaneous generation. However, it was difficult to convince people that spontaneous generation never occurred—nothing is harder than to prove a negative.

Pasteur used swan-necked glass flasks in his studies of spontaneous generation. He found that air could pass into the flasks, but the tiny organisms that were carried in the air could not pass through the necks and contaminate the broth inside.

In 1862, Pasteur was elected to the Academy of Sciences. His speeches and lectures at this time contain many wise and memorable passages. Here is an example: "A man of science should think of what will be said of him in the following century, not of the insults or compliments of one day." In January 1864, he declared: "Might not the diseases of wines be caused by organized ferments, by microscopic vegetations, the germs of which would develop when the temperature, atmospheric pressure, and exposure to air would favor their growth in wines?" He was, of course, quite right. Later that year he accepted the offer of the town of Arbois to study wine diseases.

These were a serious economic problem. Pasteur found that by keeping the wine for a short time at a temperature of 122° to 140° Fahrenheit (50° to 60° Celsius), the diseases could be prevented, and the treatment did not harm the wine. This became standard practice in wine-growing districts—it was the first example of what we now call "pasteurization."

TEXT-DEPENDENT QUESTIONS

1. For what discovery was Pasteur awarded the Red Ribbon of the Legion of Honour?
2. What is spontaneous generation?
3. To what prestigious organization was Pasteur elected in 1862?

RESEARCH PROJECT

You can duplicate Pasteur's experiment on spontaneous generation with items you can find at home. You'll need two glass mason jars with lids and an apple, cut into pieces. Carefully heat the mason jars in boiling water for a few minutes, then set them on a table. Put a few pieces of apple into one jar and quickly tighten the lid. Put a few pieces of apple into the other jar, but don't put the lid on—leave it open. Put both the sealed and open jars together on a shelf, and let them sit for two weeks. Then, take a look at the two jars: Are there differences in the fruit inside each jar? Write a one-page paper with your findings and share it with your class.

Silkworms feed on a mulberry plant. Disease threatened to destroy silkworm populations in the nineteenth century.

WORDS TO UNDERSTAND

antiseptic—a substance that will prevent growth of microbes without necessarily killing them.

cholera—a specific infection of the small intestine due to a bacillus.

flacherie—a disease that affects silkworms.

pébrine—an infectious disease of silkworms caused by a parasite.

suppuration—the production of pus in infected tissues.

CHAPTER **3**

Investigations

In 1865 the French silk industry was almost ruined by a serious epidemic of disease among the silkworms. Leaders of the industry asked Jean-Baptiste Dumas, who by that time was a member of the French Senate, for help. Dumas urged Pasteur to study the problem and try to solve it.

Pasteur hesitated. This was a completely new field for him, he pointed out, and he did not want to leave his department and laboratory in the university. Nonetheless Pasteur allowed himself to be persuaded, and in 1865 he departed for Alès, in southern France.

The silkworm disease was a fatal infection. A symptom was the appearance of tiny dark spots that looked like pepper grains on the exterior of an infected silkworm. Therefore, the disease was called **pébrine**, a word derived from *pébré*, the provincial name for pepper. In 1849 there had been a disastrous epidemic in France that wiped out most silkworms. The disease gradually spread over the next few years to affect silkworms in Europe and Asia. By 1864, healthy silkworm eggs could only be found in Japan.

Working Through Personal Tragedies

Pasteur started work in Alès trying to grow some microbes from the affected silkworms. No sooner had he begun than he received a telegram telling him that his father was desperately ill. He rushed to Arbois but arrived too late. His father was dead.

Pasteur returned in grief to his studies at Alès. He looked at hundreds of silk chrysalises and moths under the microscope and saw that many of them were diseased. The idea came to him that the disease started in the more mature forms of the worms, which produced diseased eggs, which in turn gave rise to diseased chrysalises and moths.

He obtained some healthy moths from Turkey, and decided to compare the moths hatched from their eggs with those hatched from diseased eggs.

In the meantime, he went back to his work in Paris, where a further blow struck him. His youngest child, Camille, only two years old, was seriously ill. She died in September 1865, after Pasteur had returned to Arbois.

This was perhaps the most productive period in Pasteur's life. He was busy on many important problems; he was playing a leading role in academic and scientific life and he wrote many important papers and articles.

All this time Pasteur was obsessed by the possibility of finding a connecting link between the "fermentations" or infections that attacked yeasts, those that attacked animals such as moths, and those that attacked human beings.

As usual, his general speculations were interrupted by a crisis. In 1865, **cholera** had traveled from Egypt to Marseilles and then to Paris, and in October that year

The larvae feast on mulberry leaves

To learn how silkworms produce silk, scan here:

Pasteur used this compound microscope to study the diseases of silkworms in the 1860s. It is shown with a string of silkworm cocoons.

more than 200 people were dying from it every day. Claude Bernard, Pasteur, and chemist Henri Étienne Sainte-Claire Deville were determined to find out if a microbe caused the disease. They went into the attics of a hospital, just above the cholera ward, and sampled the air. However, they did not grow any microbes that might have caused the disease. They then took blood from cholera patients and cultured it, but did not grow any microbes from these specimens either.

This work also was interrupted by a flattering invitation from the French Emperor Napoléon III to come and spend a weekend at the Palace of Compiègne. The emperor loved science, and Pasteur felt he had to accept. The emperor gave Pasteur particular attention, and spent much time in private talks with him.

During one of these conversations, Napoléon and the Empress Eugénie told Pasteur they were surprised that he did not try to make money from his work.

Pasteur replied: "In France, scientists would consider they lowered themselves by doing so." He was convinced that a man of science would complicate his life, interrupt the flow of his thoughts, and risk paralyzing his inventive faculties if he tried to make money from his discoveries. The conflict would be too deep.

In 1866 the Ministry of Agriculture asked Pasteur to continue his studies on silkworm disease. Pasteur agreed and went away again to the silk producing districts with two colleagues. The three men began by looking for a suitable house where they could set up a laboratory. They found one; it was large enough to hold Pasteur, his family and his pupils. On her way to Alès, Pasteur's daughter Cécile, then twelve years old, fell ill with typhoid fever. She died on May 23, 1866, after a sudden relapse.

Portrait of the French Emperor Napoléon III, c. 1865.

After this further calamity, Pasteur returned in sorrow to his research. He put forward the suggestion, which was new at the time, that the silkworm disease was infectious, and said that no eggs should be used that came from infected moths. He was soon able to show that infection might occur in one of two ways—either by direct contact between the worms on the same frame, or by soiling of their food by the infected excreta of the worms.

In the meantime, Pasteur was editing his book on wines. In order to keep wines free from all germs of disease and make them suitable for storage and for export, he had already shown that it was enough to heat them

This model illustrates an experiment performed in 1862 by Louis Pasteur to study the fermentation of grape juice. One bunch of grapes is wrapped in sterilized cotton wool, while the other is exposed to the air. When both bunches were ripe, they were crushed separately in vessels. Those from the covered bunch did not ferment, but the uncovered ones did. This experiment showed that alcoholic fermentation only happens when the grape juice comes into contact with germs of yeast in the air.

by the simple process that had become known as pasteurization. Pasteur did not pay much attention to the talk of old gourmets who said that heating harmed the wines and prevented them from mellowing with age. The aging of wines, said Pasteur, is due not to fermentation but to slow oxidation, which is in fact encouraged by the heating.

Funds for Future Research

All this time Pasteur was suffering from a lack of money for his research. He wrote to Napoléon asking for a larger laboratory and more money. The very next day the emperor wrote to Victor Duruy, the minister of Public Instruction, strongly supporting Pasteur's request. Duruy agreed and began to draw up plans. Meanwhile Pasteur was invited to Orleans to give a public lecture on his studies on vinegar. This took place on Monday, November 11, 1866. Pasteur was then the youngest member of the Academy of Science. An account in the local paper describes the scene: "He was of medium height, his face pale, his eyes very bright through his glasses, scrupulously neat in his dress, with a tiny rosette of the Legion of Honour in his buttonhole."

In his famous lecture, Pasteur showed that the transformation of wine into vinegar was due to a microscopic fungus, *Mycoderma aceti*. He demonstrated that the *mycoderma* would multiply profusely in any alcoholic and slightly acid liquid, and would cover a large area of liquid in forty-eight hours. Floating on the surface, the *mycoderma* absorbed oxygen from the air, transforming the alcohol into acetic acid.

The year 1867 shows Pasteur, then forty-five years old, at the height of his powers. He would start work early in the morning, working on a single problem for several hours. He was thoughtful, almost dreamy, until some action was called for when he at once revealed himself as a man of action. His intuition and imagination were as keen as those of any poet.

At the end of the year, Pasteur heard to his consternation that money had been refused for the building of his new laboratory, at a time when millions of francs were being spent on the Opera House. He prepared an article for the *Moniteur*, the official newspaper, protesting at the cuts made and contrasting the poverty of science in France with the large sums devoted to this cause in Germany, Russia, England, Austria, Bavaria, and Italy.

The article attacked the government and the editor of the *Moniteur* became alarmed. He knew that Pasteur would never agree to make any alterations, but advised him to show the proofs to Étienne Conti, secretary to Napoléon III. Conti felt that the article could not appear in the *Moniteur*, but suggested that Pasteur publish it as a booklet. Pasteur's campaign had a good effect. From that time onward, the emperor consulted him and other leading scientists about the best way to support science in France. The emperor approved of Pasteur's general argument, as did high-ranking government officials like Duruy.

In 1868 the University of Bonn offered Pasteur the degree of medical doctor for his work on microbes. Pasteur was delighted and flattered. He greatly admired German higher education, with the liberal support it received, and the intellectual independence of the university teachers.

In July 1868 Pasteur heard that the building of his laboratory was about to begin at last. His life was now very full. The results of his experiments on silkworm disease were being actively applied by the silk industry, and those on the spoilage of wine and beer by the brewers. These results were confirmed by a

GOLD MEDAL

In 1867, the French government decided to award Pasteur a special Grand Prize medal at the Exposition Universelle, a world's fair held in Paris. The award was conferred on Pasteur for his work on wine. The ceremony took place on July 1, 1867, when Paris looked its best. The central avenue of the Tuileries Gardens, the Place de la Concorde, and the Avenue des Champs Elysées were lined with soldiers. The imperial carriage drawn by eight horses, escorted by the guards in their pale blue uniforms and by the lancers of the household, arrived in triumphant array. Many royals and notables from different countries accompanied the French emperor. Another of the eminent men honored that day was Ferdinand de Lesseps, builder of the Suez Canal.

The Exposition Universelle ran from April 1 to October 31, 1867. There were over 50,000 exhibits at the fair, and forty-two nations were represented, including Great Britain, the United States, and Canada. It was the largest world's fair held up to that time, drawing more than 9.2 million visitors.

decisive experiment organized by Monsieur de Lapparent, the director of Naval Construction in the Ministry of Marine. A frigate started on a cruise around the world with a large cargo of wine. This had been heated by Pasteur to kill the *mycoderma* and so prevent spoilage. After the long journey, the wine was perfect. This demonstrated clearly that it was now possible to ship French wines all over the world without fear of deterioration.

A Sudden Illness

On October 19, 1868, Pasteur was due to read a treatise to the Academy of Science. In the morning he felt sick, with a strange tingling on the left side of his body. After lunch he had an alarming shivering fit, but insisted on going to the meeting of the academy. Madame Pasteur was uneasy about his condition, and went with him as far as the entrance of the institute.

Pasteur read the paper in his usual steady voice and walked back to his home. After a light dinner, he went to bed early. As soon as he got into bed, he felt himself attacked by the same symptoms as earlier in the day. He tried, at first in vain, to speak, but after a few moments he was able to call for help. At once Madame Pasteur sent for their friend Dr. Godélier. Pasteur explained his symptoms, which were those of a gradually increasing cerebral hemorrhage. This rapidly brought complete paralysis of the left side of his body.

For the next few days, Pasteur struggled for his life. At times it was thought that there was no hope for him. However, he gradually improved, though the paralysis remained.

All through his illness, Pasteur's mind remained clear and lucid, in contrast to his crippled body. His chief regret was that he would die before having completely solved the question of silkworm diseases. During the height of his illness, he dictated notes on this and other problems to the friends who hardly left his bedside.

Pasteur was not expected to recover, and the building work on his new laboratory slowed down and almost stopped. When he heard about this, Pasteur complained to Napoléon, who personally instructed Monsieur Duruy to make sure that the construction schedule would not suffer.

By November 30, Pasteur had improved enough to get out of bed and spend an hour in his armchair. He coolly and calmly took stock of his situation.

He was almost forty-six years old and had been working more effectively than ever, but he was now partly paralyzed. He told his wife and daughter he was anxious not to be a burden to them. His chief wish was to carry on with his work.

Most striking was the contrast between his ardent, aspiring, and active brain, and his stricken, paralyzed body. He read a lot—the works of Blaise Pascal, Pierre Nicole, and Jacques-Bénigne Bossuet. The book *Self-Help* (1859), by

Drawing of Louis Pasteur in the 1860s.

Samuel Smiles, interested and helped him greatly. His family and friends read to him in the daytime. Many friends visited him. The bulletins continued to tell of his recovery.

Pasteur was not the man to stay at home as a convalescent a moment longer than necessary. Exactly three months after his stroke, he set out for Alès to see how the work on silkworm disease was going on. A laboratory was improvised, and from his sofa or his bed Pasteur directed experiments and was able to look through his microscope to see the results. The movements of his leg and arm slowly improved.

By the season of 1869, Pasteur was eager to develop proof that the silkworm disease was due to a preventable infection. He sent four samples of eggs to

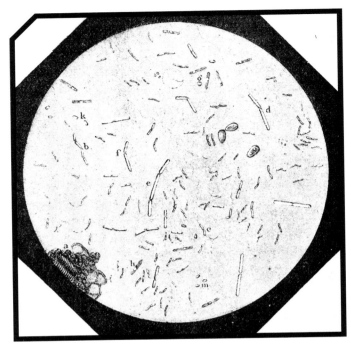

the Silk Commission of Lyons. One was healthy, and Pasteur predicted that it would hatch normally. The second was infected and Pasteur predicted that all the insects would die of pébrine. The third was infected with another disease called **flacherie**. Pasteur predicted that this too would perish. The fourth was a mixture of eggs infected with pébrine and flacherie.

The results were just as Pasteur predicted, and the Lyons Commission generously acknowledged that the scourge that had affected their industry for so long was really about to be conquered at last.

The Franco-Prussian War

In 1869, Jean-Baptiste Philibert Vaillant, a marshal of France and a senator, arranged for Pasteur to go for a long stay to one of the royal estates, the Villa Vicentina near Trieste. The aged Marshal Vaillant was close to the emperor, and was an old friend of Pasteur. He encouraged Pasteur to conduct an experiment on silkworm disease at the Villa Vicentina. The beautiful and peaceful villa would be ideal for Pasteur's convalescence.

The long journey had to be taken in short stages, as Pasteur was still a sick man. On arrival Pasteur set to work on his experiment. It was successful.

The government wished to do for Pasteur what it had already done for his famous predecessors Dumas and Claude Bernard; namely to give him a seat in the Senate. The complicated arrangements for this were started. Meanwhile Pasteur and his family spent the winter of 1869–70 at the Villa Vicentina, where his strength improved from day to day.

German soldiers escort captured French troops during the Franco-Prussian War of 1870–71. When the war began, France had a greater population than the German states, so most observers expected the French to be victorious. However, Prussia's innovations in military training and weaponry resulted in a decisive victory.

On his way home, Pasteur spent two days in Strasbourg. The city was full of rumors about the coming war with Germany. Those who knew the situation well were aware that the Prussians had been building up their army for some time, but that France had sadly neglected her defenses.

Pasteur was alarmed at the threat to his country and to his work. On his return to Paris, he found that his son had enlisted, as had every one of the students of the Ecole Normale. Pasteur wished to join the National Guard, and had to be reminded that his paralysis rendered him unfit for active service.

When the war started, Pasteur continued his work. His friends strongly advised him to leave Paris, which was threatened with a siege. On September 5, 1870,

Medical workers treat wounded French and German soldiers after the Battle of Gravelotte in August 1870, a major battle of the Franco-Prussian War. Due to unsanitary conditions, many wounded solders developed infections that proved fatal.

he reluctantly started for Arbois. He tried to get solace from his beloved books. However, the misfortunes that were daily befalling France were too much of a distraction. He found it very hard to settle down to any useful work while Paris was being encircled by an overwhelming force of Prussian soldiers.

The Franco-Prussian War brought tragedy and cruelty on a vast scale to France. There was not enough food for the starving population of Paris, and thousands of children died of starvation and infection. In surgery a new era—the era of **antiseptics**—had begun, but the brilliant work of Lister and his followers had not yet reached the French Army surgeons, who were in any case overwhelmed by the huge numbers of casualties. The wounds of many of the soldiers and civilians injured during the siege of Paris became infected. Many of them died of **suppuration**.

The Prussians showed no mercy for humanity or for culture. On January 8, 1871, the Prussian Army bombarded the Museum of Natural History in Paris. On learning about the bombardment, Pasteur sent his diploma of doctor of medicine back to the University of Bonn. He wrote, "The sight of the parchment is hateful to me and I feel offended at seeing my name, with the qualification of *Virum Clarissimum* that you have given it, placed under a name which is from now on an object of loathing to my country, that of Kaiser Wilhelm." He continued, "My conscience calls on me to ask you to remove my name from the archives of your Faculty and to take back the diploma, as a symbol of the indignation inspired in a French scientist by the barbarity and hypocrisy of the man who persists in the massacre of two great nations in order to satisfy his criminal pride."

Pasteur's son was in the defeated Eastern Army Corps, which was now returning in disorder from the front. Was he alive or dead? And where was he to be found? Pasteur went to look for him among the straggling retreating soldiers. By great good fortune he came upon him, ill, in a rough cart on the road.

Pasteur went to Geneva with his son, who recovered from his illness and went back to France to rejoin his regiment in the early days of February 1871. By now an armistice had been signed with the Germans and Pasteur wanted to return to Paris. Before he could get there, civil war broke out, and the Commune took over the government of the city.

After studying issues of beer brewing in London, Pasteur developed theories about fermentation that proved to be accurate.

Fermentation Explained

Pasteur returned to his research on the fermentation of beer. In September 1871 he visited London for the first time to study beer production in England. He was very courteously received and soon convinced the British that the reason beer became spoiled was due to infection of the yeasts.

On leaving London, Pasteur returned to Paris, where his old friend Bertin welcomed him with delight. Paris was slowly recovering from the wounds of war and civil war, and at last Pasteur was able to settle down again to his laboratory work.

After more studies, Pasteur laid down three important principles about beer spoilage:

1. Every alteration of either the wort or the beer itself is due to the development of microbes, which are the cause of the disease.

2. These microbes are brought in by the air, by the ingredients of the beer, or by the apparatus used in breweries.

3. Beer that contains no living germs is not subject to disease, and will not deteriorate.

These principles were accepted all over the world. Just as heating could preserve wine from deterioration due to various causes, so could bottled beer be preserved by being brought to a temperature of 122° to 131 °F (50–55 °C). This process became known as pasteurization and of course it is widely used to this day. Most people are familiar with pasteurized milk, which has undergone a similar treatment in order to destroy any microbes it may contain.

Pasteur foresaw that his work on infections of beer would have important applications to human disease. In his book on beer, he wrote: "When we see beer and wine undergoing profound changes because they have given refuge to microbes which have been introduced invisibly, and which are now swarming within them, it is impossible not to be haunted by the thought that similar processes may, indeed must, take place in animals and man." In this way the germ theory of infectious diseases was born.

At about this time, the German chemist Justus von Liebig disputed Pasteur's statement that the change from wine to vinegar was due to the action of a yeast called *Mycoderma aceti*. This led to a long controversy. So also did Pasteur's contention that the conversion of grape juice to alcohol—the production of wine—was due to *Mycoderma vini*. This was the name of the yeast that fermented the alcohol.

Pasteur found that some yeasts were aerobic: creatures for whose life and development air—or rather, oxygen—was necessary. Others were anaerobic and lived without oxygen. While some microbes were either aerobic or anaerobic and could not be converted to the other form of existence, there were others that could live either way. Into this group came the yeasts of fermentation. They are called "facultative anaerobes." "Fermentation," said Pasteur, "is life without air."

This new theory raised yet another chorus of controversy. Eventually, however, Pasteur's views were accepted and it became possible to lay down some new facts about the causes of fermentation, such as the following:

1. That ferments are living microbes;
2. that each kind of fermentation is caused by a different microbe; and
3. that these microbes do not arise spontaneously, but develop from other microbes that are already in existence.

TEXT-DEPENDENT QUESTIONS

1. What crisis interrupted Pasteur's work in 1865?
2. What two things did Pasteur discover about the spread of silkworm disease?
3. Why did Pasteur return the doctoral degree he had been granted by the University of Bonn?
4. What is pasteurization?

 RESEARCH PROJECT

Using the internet or your school library, find out more about the causes of the Franco-Prussian War of 1870–71. In a two-page paper, explain the main factors that led to conflict and draw a conclusion about whether or not the war could have been avoided. Use examples to support your conclusion. Share your findings with your class.

After developing a process to make food and drinks safer by heating them to kill harmful bacteria, Pasteur shifted the focus of his work to the relationship of germs, diseases, and infections.

WORDS TO UNDERSTAND

bacilli—rod-shaped microbes.

butyric acid—an organic acid found in butter and other substances.

carbolic acid—the name of a strongly disinfectant chemical substance.

malignant pustule—sore in the skin, that occur from anthrax infection.

pus—a fluid mixture of white blood cells, other body cells, and microbes produced in infected tissues.

sepsis—infection of living tissue.

septicemia—infection of the bloodstream.

vaccine—substance that generally includes a weakened or mutated form of a disease, which can be used to protect people from the disease.

CHAPTER 4

Treating Wounds and Diseases

After his work on yeasts, Pasteur decided to study the causes of infectious disease. Many factors drove him to work in this field—his natural humanity, the memory of the children he had lost, and compassionate thoughts of the thousands of young men and women who every year fell victim to the diseases caused by microscopic germs.

Pasteur deeply regretted that he was not a medical man. If he had been, his task would have been much easier, since of course he had to work with medical doctors and persuade them about the truth of his ideas. Fortunately, at the beginning of 1873, an unexpected vacancy occurred in the Academy of Medicine. Pasteur was elected, and this helped to make up for his lack of a medical degree.

As soon as Pasteur was elected, he determined to be a most conscientious and punctual academician. His pleasure in his election was much increased by the fact that he would be joining his great friend and colleague Claude Bernard. For a long time, the latter had been saddened by the hostility of doctors who worked in hospitals toward those who worked in laboratories.

Claude Bernard was convinced that the application of experimental science would enable medicine to emerge from quackery. "We shall not live to see the blossoming out of scientific medicine," he said, "But such is the fate of humanity. Those who sow seeds on the fields of science are not destined to reap the fruits of their labours."

German bacteriologist Robert Koch (1843–1910) discovered the bacillus that causes tuber-culosis in 1882.

It is indeed difficult for us to get inside the minds of medical people at the time. In the years 1865 to 1869, Jean-Antoine Villemin proved that tuberculosis was a disease that reproduced itself, and could not be reproduced except by itself. In other words, it was specific and contagious, and could be transmitted from one sick person to another. He was treated by most of the rather conservative medical profession as if he were a wild revolutionary. In fact, he was a quiet, modest and gentle man.

Villemin had not discovered the bacillus of tuberculosis. This was not achieved until later by Robert Koch in 1882. But Villemin suspected that such a germ existed. He experimented on animals, inoculating them with tubercular material. He took the sputum of tuberculosis patients, spread it on cotton wool, dried it, and then made the cotton wool into a bed for young guinea pigs, which contracted the disease soon afterward.

His opponent, Hermann Pidoux, ridiculed Villemin's ideas, which resembled Pasteur's picture of germs floating about in the air. "Is it not better," said Pidoux, "to follow the truer and more philosophical doctrine of spontaneous decay? Tuberculosis is due to the spontaneous decay of the body under the influence of

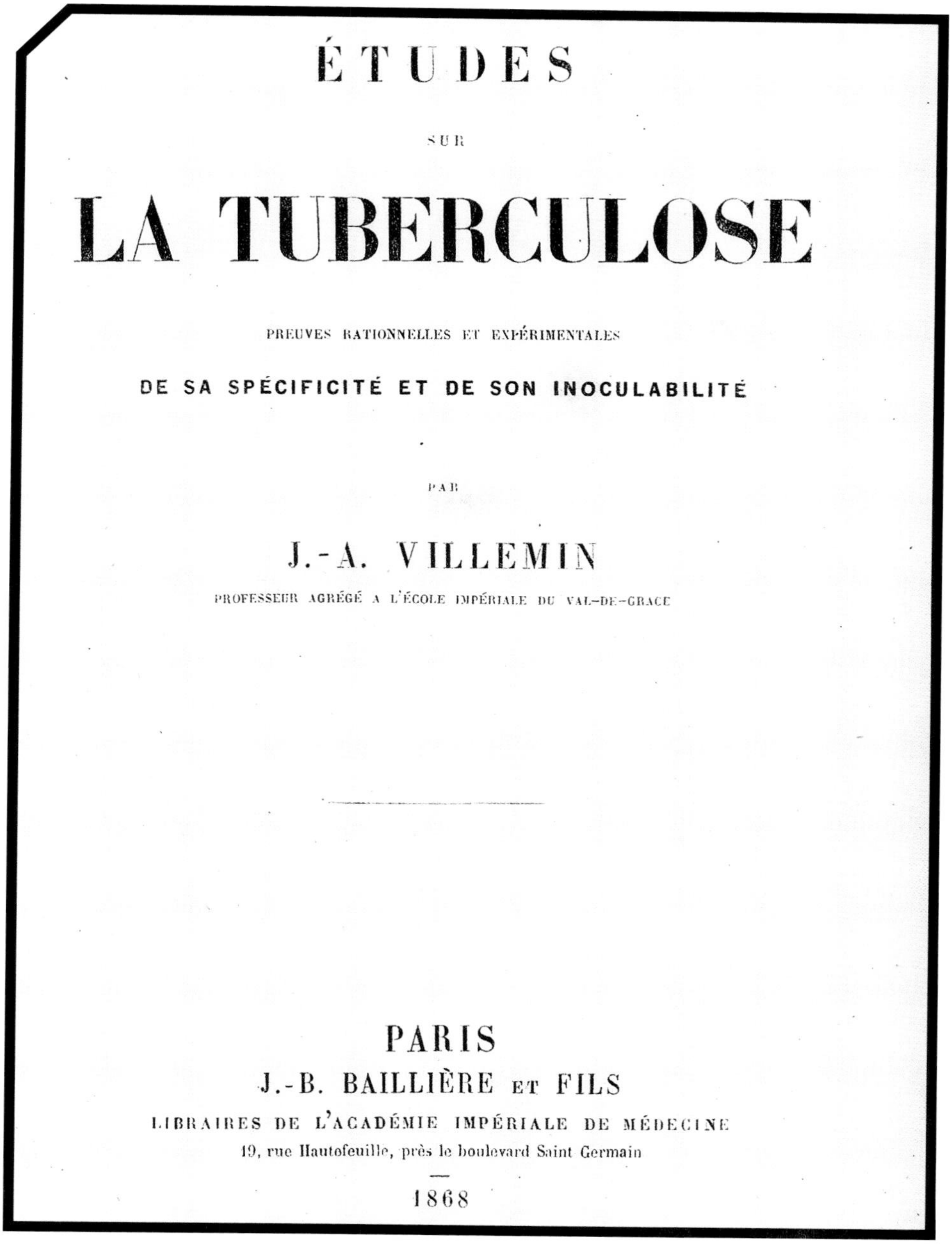

ÉTUDES

SUR

LA TUBERCULOSE

PREUVES RATIONNELLES ET EXPÉRIMENTALES

DE SA SPÉCIFICITÉ ET DE SON INOCULABILITÉ

PAR

J.-A. VILLEMIN

PROFESSEUR AGRÉGÉ A L'ÉCOLE IMPÉRIALE DU VAL-DE-GRACE

PARIS

J.-B. BAILLIÈRE ET FILS

LIBRAIRES DE L'ACADÉMIE IMPÉRIALE DE MÉDECINE

19, rue Hautefeuille, près le boulevard Saint Germain

1868

In his 1868 book Etudes sur la Tuberculose (Studies on Tuberculosis), *Jean-Antoine Villemin (1827–92) proposed that an unknown germ caused tuberculosis. However, scientists who believed in spontaneous generation ridiculed his findings.*

PROPHETIC STATEMENT

Armand Trousseau (1801–67) was a French doctor and teacher who developed revolutionary methods to treat several diseases, including emphysema, croup, and malaria. In one of his final speeches, delivered to the Academy of Medicine some five years before the controversy in the French scientific community over the cause of infection erupted, Trousseau prophetically proposed a theory. "The great theory of ferments is therefore now connected with an organic function; every ferment is a germ, the life of which is manifested by a special secretion. It may be that

Armand Trousseau

it is so for morbid viruses; they may be ferments, which, deposited within the organism at a given moment and under determined circumstances, manifest themselves by divers products. So will the variolous ferment [smallpox] produce variolic fermentation, giving birth to thousands of pustules, and likewise the virus of glanders, that of sheep pox, etc.... Other viruses appear to act locally, but, nevertheless, they ultimately modify the whole organism, as do gangrene, **malignant pustula**, contagious erysipelas, etc. May it not be supposed, under such circumstances, that the ferment or organized matter of those viruses can be carried about by the lancet, the atmosphere or the linen bandages?"

numerous causes, which we have to look for everywhere to cut down the evil to its roots."

Pidoux commented sarcastically on Villemin's theory that tuberculosis was due to a microbe: "Then all we doctors have to do is to set our nets to catch the germs of tuberculosis and find a **vaccine**!" As it turned out, this remark was quite correct.

The Healing of Wounds

People in different branches of medicine and veterinary work now began to think about Pasteur's theories of infectious disease, and to apply them to their own work.

Casmir Davaine, a French doctor, was studying anthrax, a very serious disease of farm animals that resulted in **septicemia**, or infection of the bloodstream. Davaine had observed that the blood of the sick animals contained small parasites that were visible under a microscope. These were the anthrax **bacilli**. After studying Pasteur's writings, Davaine concluded that these bacteria were the cause of the disease.

Scan here for a short video on the development of germ theory:

A doctor poses with two soldiers wounded during the Franco-Prussian War, 1870. They were among the fortunate few who survived surgery.

Davaine was violently attacked for his views. The old guard still maintained that putrid infection was not due to living germs. They believed that the putrid odors—known as "miasma"—caused the disease.

The controversy grew and many leading doctors took part. The traditional hospital doctors ridiculed the ideas of scientists, who, they said, should know and keep to their place in the scheme of things. This was a humble place. "Laboratory surgery has destroyed very many animals and saved very few human beings," a well-known surgeon named Édouard Chassaignac said in a speech to the Academy of Medicine. "Laboratory results should be brought out in a careful, modest and reserved manner."

Looking back at this violent controversy, we can see that Pasteur was one of a band of forward-looking doctors, who were all thinking the same way. As always in science, progress is not made by the efforts of a single individual, but by the change of the climate of opinion brought about by advances made by all the leaders in the field.

Speaking in the academy, Pasteur recalled his own experiments on lactic and **butyric** fermentations and on beer. Beer was altered by the presence of microbes infecting the yeasts. If beer becomes altered, it is because it contains organized ferments—microbes. "The correlation between the disease and the presence of microbes is certain, and indisputable. So it is with human disease."

Today we have largely overcome septic infection in hospitals. If such cases occur at all, they are unusual. There is an elaborate routine, and a complicated organization, to prevent them.

But in Pasteur's time it was quite different. Hospitals were hotbeds of infection. During the war of 1870, it was agonizing for any sensitive person to work in the casualty wards. The wounds of all the patients were suppurating; a horrible stink pervaded the atmosphere and infectious septicemia was all over the place. "**Pus** seemed to germinate everywhere, as if it had been sown by the surgeon," wrote a medical student of the time named Landouzy.

Charles-Pierre Denonvilliers, a surgeon, said to his pupils, "When an amputation seems necessary, think ten times before you decide to do it. Too often, when we decide upon an operation we are just signing the patient's death warrant." For the wound would almost certainly become infected; the patient would develop septicemia, and die. We must remember that this was long before the days of penicillin and other antibiotics that we now take for granted. Doctors then had no effective way of treating serious infections.

During the siege of Paris, the famous surgeon Auguste Nélaton worked in the Grand Hôtel, which had been converted into a hospital. He was in despair as he witnessed the death of almost every patient who had been operated on. "He who conquers purulent infection would deserve a golden statue," he declared.

At the end of the war, Alphonse Guérin observed: "Perhaps the cause of purulent infection may be the germs or ferments discovered by Pasteur to exist in the air. If miasmas are ferments, I might protect the wounded from their fatal influence by filtering the air, as Pasteur did. The idea of cotton wool dressings then came to me and I had the satisfaction of seeing my anticipations realized."

Guérin's method was as follows: he arrested the bleeding, ligatured the blood vessels, and carefully washed the wound with a **carbolic acid** solution or with alcohol mixed with camphor. Then he applied layers of cotton wool, binding the wound with linen bandages. He left the dressings for about twenty days.

Out of thirty-four patients treated in this way in June 1871, nineteen survived. Surgeons were amazed at this survival rate. They could hardly believe it. A French doctor named Paul Reclus wrote, "We had grown to look on purulent infection as an inevitable and necessary disease, an almost divinely instituted consequence of any important operation."

Even more dangerous than atmospheric germs were what were called "contagium germs," such as the surgeon's hands, sponges, and instruments. Infinite precautions have to be taken against them today; they were not even thought of then. Filthy used dressings were left lying about in contact with vessels used in surgical operations. During the Franco-Prussian War, surgeons began to wash wounds carefully and reduced the frequency of dressings. Even these simple measures produced better results.

In 1873 Guérin invited Pasteur to see his methods. Pasteur gladly accepted. This was the beginning of a new period in which he made many visits to hospitals, and had practical discussions with his medical colleagues.

Pasteur was delighted at the thought that he been a means of awakening in other people ideas likely to lead to the good of humanity. This joy was increased by a letter he received from Joseph Lister early in 1874. Lister was Professor of Surgery in Edinburgh. He was a thoughtful man, who read a great deal of medical and scientific literature. For years he had been trying to find a way to reduce the numbers of his patients who developed **sepsis** after operations, all too often with fatal results. He had come to the conclusion that sepsis was due to the putrefaction of wounds by microbes.

Scottish doctor Joseph Lister (1827–1912) developed antiseptic surgical practices that prevented infection. Pasteur's research on fermentation and the process of decay inspired Lister to develop his sterile procedures.

In Lister's wards the instruments, sponges, and all the other articles used in dressings were dipped before use in a strong solution of carbolic acid. The surgeon and his assistants scrubbed and rinsed their hands in a weak carbolic acid solution. During every operation, a carbolic acid spray was applied to the wound. After the operation, the wound was again washed with carbolic solution. Antiseptic materials were used for dressings.

A French medical student, Lucas-Championnière, described Lister's methods in French medical journals and later became an exponent of them. The first principles of defense against gangrene, he said, were "extreme and minute

LISTER'S LETTER TO PASTEUR

Following is the text of a letter that Joseph Lister wrote to Louis Pasteur in 1874, explaining how the French scientist's discoveries had informed Lister's methods to prevent infection during surgeries:

Allow me to beg your acceptance of a pamphlet, which I sent by the same post, containing an account of some investigations into the subject, which you have done so much to elucidate, the germ theory of fermentative changes. I flatter myself that you may read with some interest what I have written on the organisms which you were the first to describe in your Study on the lactic fermentation.

I do not know whether the records of British Surgery ever meet your eye. If so, you will have seen from time to time notices of the antiseptic system of treatment, which I have been labouring for the last nine years to bring to perfection.

Allow me to take this opportunity to tender you my most cordial thanks for having, by your brilliant researches, demonstrated to me the truth of the germ theory of putrefaction, and thus furnished me with the principle upon which alone the antiseptic system can be carried out. Should you at any time visit Edinburgh it would, I believe, give you sincere gratification to see at our hospital how largely mankind is being benefited by your labours.

I need hardly add that it would afford me the highest gratification to show you how greatly surgery is indebted to you.

Forgive the freedom with which a common love of science inspires me, and believe me, with profound respect,

Yours very sincerely, Joseph Lister

care in the dressing of wounds." However, nobody took much notice of him, or of a lecture given by Lister in France at the beginning of 1870. The heads of the profession there, as elsewhere, had absolute confidence in themselves and few people at that time showed any interest in the rumors of success obtained by the antiseptic method. Yet between 1867 and 1869, thirty-four of Lister's patients out of forty had survived amputation—success that was quite unprecedented.

Even in his own country, Lister was violently attacked. He let the stupid critics talk away and replied by painstakingly improving his methods. With calm courage and smiling kindliness, he tested each step carefully, going over every detail. Like Pasteur, Lister was a man of the greatest fortitude, determination and courage. Pasteur was delighted to find such an ally. He enthusiastically adopted Lister's teachings and did his best to pass them on to others.

Pasteur's experiments have a very modern air. "To demonstrate the bad effects of ferments and microbes on the suppuration of wounds, I would make two identical wounds on two symmetrical limbs of an animal under chloroform," he wrote. "To one of these I would apply a cotton wool dressing with every possible precaution. On the other I would place microbes taken from a septic wound.

"I should like to cut open a wound on an animal under chloroform in a very carefully selected part of the body and in absolutely pure air, that is, air quite free from any kind of germ, after which I would maintain a pure atmosphere around the wound," Pasteur continued. "I am inclined to think that perfect healing would follow under such conditions, for there would be nothing to hinder the work of repair and organization which must be completed on the surface of a wound if it is to heal." This is, of course, an account of aseptic, as distinct from antiseptic, surgery.

Pasteur patiently showed the advantages of taking infinite precautions for cleanliness and destroying infectious germs. His struggles in the Academy of Medicine were long and painful, but eventually he succeeded in convincing his colleagues.

In 1874 Dr. J. David Roger, the annual secretary of the Academy of Medicine, applied to the government for a special grant for Pasteur to enable him to continue his experiments into "the infinitely small." The bill was passed by a huge

By the 1870s, Louis Pasteur was internationally renowned as a medical researcher.

majority. This was only the third time in the nineteenth century that the government had made such a special grant.

Thereafter Pasteur's annuity relieved him from all financial worry, and recompensed him for having to give up his professorship at the Sorbonne owing to ill health. He was working at the Ecole Normale, leading a normal, calm life.

In 1876 he went to an International Congress of Silk Culture in Milan and took the opportunity to visit many institutes where his methods of protecting silkworms from disease had been adopted. It was a triumphant and happy voyage, in which he was welcomed everywhere as a great benefactor. At last his efforts were gaining their just rewards.

 TEXT-DEPENDENT QUESTIONS

1. Why did Pasteur decided to study the causes of infectious disease?
2. What is anthrax?
3. Who was Joseph Lister?

 RESEARCH PROJECT

Choose one of the eminent scientists mentioned in this chapter, including Jean-Antoine Villemin, Robert Koch, Casmir Davaine, Armand Trousseau, Alphonse Guérin, and Joseph Lister. Write a two-page report on this person and their scientific accomplishments.

"Louis Pasteur in his Laboratory," a painting from 1885 by Finnish artist Albert Edelfelt.

 WORDS TO UNDERSTAND

childbed fever—a bacterial infection contracted by women in childbirth.

hydrophobia—the human form of rabies.

medulla—part of the base of the brain.

rabies—a specific infectious disease contracted by humans and animals by contact with infected animals.

swine erysipelas—a specific bacterial infection of swine.

CHAPTER 5

Attacking Anthrax and Rabies

Pasteur now took up the study of a disease that French farmers called *charbon*, which today is known as anthrax. This disease was ruining agriculture in the late nineteenth century. Many French provinces lost thousands of cattle and other livestock every year. In the Beauce region of northern France, for instance, the disease killed up to 20 percent of the sheep in some years. In some parts of the Auvergne, the proportion of deaths was always at least 10 or 15 percent and sometimes it rose to 50 percent.

Animals stricken with the disease died of the acute illness within a few hours. Their blood was thickened and darker in color than normal. The spleen enlarged to an enormous size, so the disease was sometimes called "splenic fever."

Men, too, could easily catch this dangerous infection from animals. An exposed cut or scratch was often enough to pass the disease on to people that came into contact with infected livestock: shepherds, butchers, slaughterhouse workers, or farmers, for example. Even people who did not work on farms might get the infection from contaminated shaving brushes and the like. Meat porters picked up the infection from sides of meat. Women might get it from wearing clothes made from infected animals. Once contracted, the disease often caused blood poisoning, and most of the patients succumbed.

Seeking the Bacilli

As early as 1838, veterinary professor Onésime Delafond had pointed out that the blood of affected animals contained little "rods," as he called them, after observing them under a microscope. These were, of course, the bacilli of anthrax. However, most people regarded this discovery as of no importance.

A young German physician, Robert Koch, became interested in this disease in 1870. He showed that the bacilli, which were now called *Bacillus anthracis*, would produce the disease when inoculated into guinea pigs, rabbits, and mice.

Pasteur now tackled the problem. He took a small drop of blood from an animal that had died of anthrax and put it into a liquid culture medium. The resulting growth of bacteria, when injected into rabbits, produced anthrax. After

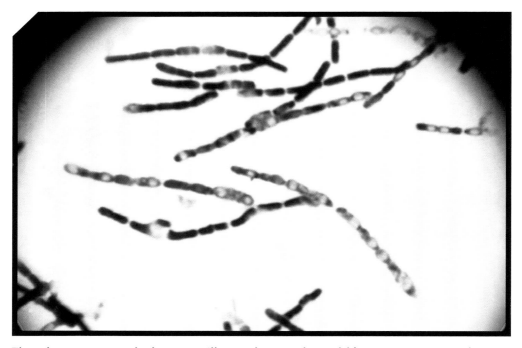

This photomicrograph shows Bacillus anthracis, *the rod-like microorganism that causes anthrax. This infectious disease occurs most commonly in cattle, sheep, goats, and other herbivores. It can also occur in humans when they are exposed to infected animals, or tissue from infected animals.*

Anthrax can be spread to humans who are exposed to infected animals. This image shows a farmer whose left forearm has a large anthrax lesion.

several more experiments, Pasteur was able to declare, "Anthrax is caused by the bacillus, just as trichinosis is caused by the trichina and itch by its special acarus—with this difference, that in anthrax the parasite can only be seen through a microscope and very much enlarged."

Pasteur's studies of animals with anthrax went on for many years. He wanted to find a way to prevent the disease. It was dangerous work—any infection in the laboratory was likely to prove fatal. Even a slight cut on the hand by a scalpel while an animal was being dissected could kill a laboratory worker. But Pasteur and his colleagues carried on, in spite of the personal danger to themselves. This is an aspect of their work that is often forgotten today, now that we have powerful medicines that can prevent diseases from developing or cure them when they are established.

During this work Pasteur coined the word "microbe" to denote the microscopic creatures that he had shown to be the cause of so many diseases. The rest of the world followed his example.

New Studies

Pasteur was now dividing his time equally between the hospital and the laboratory. He tackled every problem of infection as it arose. **Childbed fever** became another of his interests. He was now working more fruitfully and effectively than ever. His children were grown up, his sons and daughter were married, and he had several grandchildren. He had recovered well from his paralysis. He gave many lectures in institutes in various countries and published many papers and books on his experiments.

Pasteur now embarked on a new study of a farmyard infection: fowl cholera. This disease causes previously healthy chickens to die suddenly in their coops. The infected hens or roosters stagger around drowsily until they fall dead in agony.

In 1869 a veterinary surgeon named Mortiz had observed some microbes in the blood of stricken animals. Henri Toussaint, a young professor at the Toulouse Veterinary School, continued this work. Toussaint sent Pasteur the head of a

Scan here for a short video on how vaccines work:

rooster that had died of cholera and Pasteur grew the microbes from it. He showed that they produced only a mild disease in guinea pigs, which he used for further studies in the laboratories. Soon Pasteur was able to devise a culture medium that was suitable for growing the organisms in the laboratory.

Pasteur now made an important discovery. If chickens were inoculated with a laboratory culture that was only one or two days old, there was a good chance that they would develop the disease and die. One day, however, one of Pasteur's assistants injected some chickens with a culture that had been stored in a cupboard in the laboratory for a few weeks. The chickens became ill, but recovered. After they had gotten better, Pasteur injected one of his stronger fowl cholera cultures into them. The chicks did not die of the disease.

Pasteur recognized that while the neglected culture had been stored in the laboratory, something had happened to weaken it, so that it could no longer cause a fatal disease in chickens. Instead, the chicken's immune system had figured out how to fight the infection by the weakened microbe, without causing serious harm to the chicken. Once this happened, chickens were able to resist infection by the more virulent forms of the disease. This weakening of the microbe, or "attenuation," was an observation of the greatest importance. It opened the way to the possibility of preparing vaccines against microbes by growing them artificially in the laboratory and weakening them.

Pasteur saw that his observations on fowl cholera led to the possibility of preparing vaccines against other animal diseases, such as anthrax, and so conquering them. More important, the dazzling prospect opened up of protecting humanity from the epidemic diseases that were then threatening entire populations in all countries.

Pasteur plunged with enthusiasm into the work of developing vaccines, and, equally important, of convincing other scientists that his methods were worth intensive study because of their possible importance.

Anthrax Vaccine

Meanwhile, Pasteur was still studying the cause of anthrax in farm animals. One day he was on a visit to a farm near Chartres where he often went to observe the sick animals. He noticed that the soil in one place had a different color from the soil in the rest of the farm. He asked the owner of the farm if he could explain this, and the owner replied that a sheep that had died from anthrax had been buried there the previous year. Pasteur examined this ground carefully, and found that it contained many of the little cylinders of earth that earthworms deposit in the soil.

The idea at once came to Pasteur that perhaps the earthworms carried the anthrax microbes from the infected field to other areas, and so spread the disease to other animals. As usual, he wasted no time on further speculation, but decided to test this idea in his laboratory. He took back to Paris a number of earthworms from the infected soil, dissected them, and found the spores of the anthrax bacillus in the cylinders of earth in their intestines. In this way Pasteur found that earthworms could be responsible for the spread of anthrax.

Clearly, it was dangerous to bury animals that had been infected with anthrax in land where the earthworms might pick up the infection from them and convey it elsewhere. So Pasteur recommended that the corpses of animals be buried not in rich pasture meadows, but in sandy or chalky soil, which was poor and dry and unsuitable for the growth of earthworms.

There remained the problem of protecting livestock from infection, and Pasteur continued his efforts to produce a vaccine by attenuating or weakening the organisms artificially. At last, in February 1881, Pasteur believed he had succeeded. Now the vaccine had to be tested. Farmers from the agricultural society of Melun, near Paris, organized a trial, putting sixty sheep at Pasteur's disposal.

Pasteur devised his experiment in this way: twenty-five of the sheep were to be given two injections of his attenuated vaccine over a period of about two weeks. These sheep would then be injected with a very virulent anthrax culture. Twenty-five unvaccinated sheep would be injected at the same time with the same anthrax culture. These fifty animals would afterward be compared with the remaining ten sheep who had undergone no treatment at all.

"The twenty-five unvaccinated sheep will all die," Pasteur predicted, "and the vaccinated sheep will survive." Later, ten cows were added to the trial; six were to be vaccinated and four left unvaccinated.

Pasteur injects a sheep with his anthrax vaccine during the trial in Melun, France.

This crucial experiment was conducted in a full blaze of publicity, which left no room for a doubtful result. If it succeeded, Pasteur's methods would be triumphantly justified in the eyes of the world. If it failed, he would be discredited and ridiculed. But Pasteur did not flinch. His careful and painstaking work had convinced him that he would succeed.

The experiment took place in May 1881. On May 5, the test animals were given their first injection of the attenuated vaccine. The second injection of the attenuated vaccine followed twelve days later. On May 31, all the animals were inoculated with the virulent culture. Vaccinated and unvaccinated animals were separated in different fields and the anxious wait began.

On June 2, 1881, Pasteur received a telegram from Melun—all the unvaccinated animals had died of anthrax, and all the vaccinated animals were alive and well.

Pasteur rushed to Melun, where a large crowd had gathered. As he arrived at the farmyard with his young collaborators, a roar of applause broke out. His triumph was complete. Anthrax was conquered at last. Veterinary surgeons and farmers hurried to protect animals with the new method.

Honors were showered on Pasteur. The government bestowed on him the Grand Ribbon of the Legion of Honour. Then came a further triumph. In August Pasteur was invited to represent his country at the International Medical Congress in London. As he arrived at St. James's Hall, filled to overflowing with delegates from all over the world, cheers broke out. Pasteur was the great success of the Congress. Back in France, Pasteur was elected one of the "immortals" of the French Academy.

The Triumph over Rabies

The whole world began to enjoy the benefits of Pasteur's discoveries. In the year 1882, in France alone, more than half a million sheep and 80,000 oxen were vaccinated against anthrax. Farmers saved millions of francs that they had lost due to livestock deaths from disease in previous years. The great English physiologist Thomas Henry Huxley declared in a public lecture at the Royal Society in London, "Pasteur's discoveries alone would suffice to cover the war indemnity of five milliards [approximately equal to $1 billion in US currency at the time] paid by France to Germany in 1870."

Meanwhile Pasteur's previous discoveries were saving countless human lives. Since the antiseptic method had been introduced into surgery, the mortality of operations in hospitals had fallen from 50 to 5 percent. In maternity hospitals, where the mortality had previously been 10 to 20 percent, it was now less than three per thousand.

Yet problems multiplied also. **Swine erysipelas** was a disease of pigs that caused great damage, and Pasteur embarked on the study of this. Cholera was advancing in Egypt, and threatened the city of Alexandria. Pasteur went there to study it in 1883. Unexpectedly, the epidemic ceased, and Pasteur went back to France.

Another major problem presented itself, that of **rabies**. Many dogs in every country were afflicted with this fatal disease, which was a perpetual danger to human beings who might be bitten by them. People could also develop the disease without being bitten; a lick from a sick dog's tongue was enough. Nor were dogs the only dangerous animals. Wolves, jackals, and other carnivores were also

PASTEUR'S PERSONALITY

Louis Pasteur was no cold-blooded, aloof intellectual. His friend Roux once wrote: "It is a characteristic of exalted minds to put passion into ideas"—this was an excellent description of Pasteur. He had to fight ignorance, prejudice, the innate conservatism of his eminent colleagues and of the medical establishment. He fought this fight with kindness, good humor, and a basic equanimity, which yet allowed the passion of his "exalted mind" to drive him on and to inspire other men with some of his own enthusiasm.

affected and could transmit the disease to human beings in the same way.

The human version of the disease was often called **hydrophobia**, from the Greek words meaning "fear of water." It is an inflammation of the brain in which the patients become very excitable. Even the sound of running water, as from an ordinary tap, may be enough to being on an attack of morbid excitement, hence the name.

Rabies in both humans and animals was, and still is, a most serious disease; recovery is almost unheard of. It had been shown in 1870 that the infectious agent was present in the saliva of sick animals. Pasteur studied the saliva of dogs and of human beings who died of the disease, and confirmed the presence of

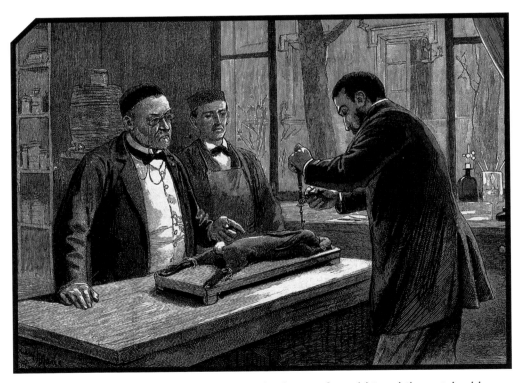

Pasteur injects the active rabies virus into the brain of a rabbit, while watched by two assistants. Chloroform was used to put animals to sleep to stop them from struggling. Once a rabbit developed rabies, it was killed and an extract from its brain was used to make the attenuated vaccine.

the infectious agent in them. He then made a crucial discovery—that the agent of rabies was also to be found in the dog's brain and spinal cord.

Was it possible to attenuate this in the same way as the anthrax bacillus had been attenuated?

Pasteur set to work. He removed the **medulla** from the brain of a rabbit that had died of rabies and suspended it in a sterilized vial for fourteen days. Pasteur then made an extract of the dried tissue and injected it into dogs. They did not develop rabies. Next day he injected the dogs with an extract of medulla which had been dried for thirteen days, and the following day with a twelve-day extract, and so on. Then he allowed these dogs to be bitten by rabid animals. The inoculated animals did not develop rabies. Pasteur's process of drying the medulla had successfully attenuated the microbe. These extracts could perhaps now be used to protect human beings and animals.

Pasteur was anxious that his findings be verified, and a special commission was set up for this purpose. Experiments conducted on numerous animals confirmed Pasteur's findings. But the question remained: Could human beings be protected in the same way?

On Monday, July 6, 1885, a nine-year-old boy named Joseph Meister entered Pasteur's laboratory with his mother. Two days before, he had been bitten by a mad dog, and the mother was distraught. Human beings never recovered once they had developed rabies; the disease was always fatal. Could anything be done to save the child?

Pasteur was not yet ready to try his vaccine on human beings. What should he do? Should he do nothing and let the boy die? Should he risk his vaccine on Joseph, who might die in any case, when Pasteur would be discredited and, very probably, blamed for the child's death? Yet he felt in his bones that his vaccine could save Joseph.

Privately, Pasteur consulted two senior medical colleagues. The doctors advised him to go ahead and vaccinate the boy. Pasteur supervised as medical professionals injected Joseph with the vaccine over a period of ten days. Joseph remained well and went home a few days after the treatment was completed.

An 1886 newspaper illustration show Pasteur examining a patient who has been bitten by a rabid animal; around him are portraits of some of the patients who came to the Pasteur Institute seeking the cure for rabies.

The news flashed around the world: Rabies was conquered. From all over Europe, farmers and peasants who had been bitten by rabid dogs and wolves began to stream into Paris to receive Pasteur's treatment. Once again, Pasteur had the courage to put his theories to the most crucial test, and had triumphed.

The Pasteur Institute

The Academy of Sciences recommended that an institute, to be known as the Pasteur Institute, be set up to organize the preventive treatment of rabies. They opened a subscription list in France and other countries. Immediately money started pouring in from all over the world. This was the beginning of what has become the most famous institute anywhere for the study of microbes and the prevention of microbial disease.

The Pasteur Institute soon extended its field of activity to other subjects in microbiology, and today remains highly respected for the quality of its research. To have worked at the Pasteur Institute became a hallmark of excellence for all young microbiologists. Today the Pasteur Institute has a network of twenty-four institutes in other countries in Africa and Asia, as well as the Pasteur Foundation in the United States. Similar institutes have also been established in other countries, such as the Lister Institute in the United Kingdom or the Centers for Disease Control in the United States.

Pasteur's many accomplishments made his name familiar all over the world. He was asked to attend and to speak at charitable and scientific gatherings in many different countries. He always agreed to do this whenever he could, for he knew

The original building of the Pasteur Institute in Paris. Today, the institute remains at the forefront of the battle against infectious disease.

that his presence was a guarantee of success. He was liberal with his help and sympathy for others, especially younger doctors and scientists. He answered countless letters from private people who wrote to him about their problems.

Pasteur moved into the new and splendid laboratories of the Pasteur Institute where he continued his experiments. He addressed meetings, wrote scientific papers, attended congresses. As the year 1892 approached, committees in various countries were set up to organize the celebrations for his seventieth birthday. The official reception was held on the morning of the actual day, December 27.

The Great Hall of the Sorbonne was crowded by notables from all over the world, including delegates from all the leading scientific societies. Pasteur entered leaning on the arm of the president of the republic, Marie François Sadi Carnot. The highlight of this occasion, never to be forgotten by those who saw it, was the moment when Pasteur and Lister embraced one another—two of the greatest scientists the world has ever known, to each of whom countless lesser mortals owed their lives. The gesture was a living symbol of the international brotherhood of science and of collaboration between the wise men of different nations.

TEXT-DEPENDENT QUESTIONS

1. What did Onésime Delafond discover in 1838 about the blood of animals infected with anthrax?
2. How did Pasteur develop a vaccine for fowl cholera?
3. What was the result of Pasteur's 1881 anthrax inoculation test?
4. What is rabies?

RESEARCH PROJECT

For some people in the United States, the issue of universal vaccination is controversial. Children today are vaccinated to protect against dozens of diseases. To prevent diseases from occurring, all members of a population must be vaccinated. However, some parents fear that there are other health issues that result from vaccination, and they have refused to have their children vaccinated. Investigate this issue using your school library or the internet. What are the issues that arise when not all children are vaccinated? Are there valid concerns about side effects of vaccines? Write a two-page report, using examples to support your conclusions.

A syringe for delivering Roux's antitoxin treatment for diphtheria.

WORDS TO UNDERSTAND

antitoxin—serum containing antibodies, antidote to toxin.

diphtheria—a specific infectious disease that used to be common in childhood.

toxin—poisonous substance.

CHAPTER 6

Final Years

Pasteur was now an old man, but he went on working with the vigor of his youth. Yet another problem presented itself, that of **diphtheria**, which every year killed thousands of children in France and other countries. During outbreaks, entire classes of children might become ill. More than half of those affected died of the disease.

The bacterium that causes the disease was discovered by a German named Klebs in 1883. In the Pasteur Institute, it was studied by Émile Roux and Alexandre Yersin, two of Pasteur's assistants. They found that cultures of the microbe contained a toxic substance, which, when injected into guinea pigs and other animals, produced in them the signs of diphtheria. This diphtheria **toxin** was the main weapon whereby the microbe produced disease in human beings.

Roux found that by adding iodine to the toxin, he could reduce its potency. He injected some of this weakened toxin into horses, and found that the horses became immune. Their blood produced an **antitoxin** that neutralized the virulent toxin.

Roux gave injections of this horse serum to other animals that had previously been infected with diphtheria bacilli. Then he injected these animals with virulent diphtheria bacilli. The animals did not develop diphtheria, or, if they had already contracted the disease, they recovered.

The next and crucial step was to see if human beings could be cured in the same way. A trial was organized at the one of the two hospitals where

Pierre Paul Émile Roux (1853–1933) was a friend and co-worker of Pasteur, and one of the founders of the Pasteur Institute.

diphtheritic children were admitted. In the other hospital, the old methods of treatment were to continue.

Within four months, after hundreds of children had been given antitoxin, the results were evident. In the treated children, the mortality of diphtheria had been brought down from 51 to 24 percent. In the others the mortality was 60 percent. This was the start of a long fight against diphtheria. Today, this once-devastating disease has virtually disappeared in the United States and other industrialized nations.

In November 1894 Pasteur became ill with kidney failure. After several weeks he slowly started to recover, and his mind, if not his body, regained its normal vigor. As soon as the weather allowed, a tent was set up for him in the garden of the Pasteur Institute, where he went to sit. However, in the spring of 1895 his strength began to diminish visibly. Soon he could hardly walk. He grew weaker and weaker and, on Friday September 27, 1895, he took to his bed for the last time. Next day he died peacefully, surrounded by his family, colleagues, and students.

The Genius of Pasteur

Circumstances produce the man—sometimes. Sometimes, however, they do not.

It is true that by the mid-nineteenth century, the accepted knowledge about microbes, and the state of medical science, were advanced enough for it to be

The Sunday, October 13, 1895, supplement to Le Petit Journal, a popular French daily newspaper, commemorates the life of Louis Pasteur.

Scientists continue Pasteur's work at the Pasteur Institute in Paris, 1910.

possible for someone to pull all these threads together, as Pasteur did. After all, he was not the first to propose the germ theory of disease, or to advocate antiseptic surgery. Yet how much more difficult would Lister's task have been had Pasteur never lived!

When we think of Pasteur's work on specific problems such as fermentation and the diseases of beer and wine, anthrax, fowl cholera, plague, and rabies—to name but a few—his influence was surely decisive. By now, no doubt, these scourges would have been almost conquered without him. But it would have taken humanity so much longer; countless more lives would have been lost, and all future history would have been different.

In Pasteur's time, vast problems of human and animal diseases were there to be solved. Pasteur was able to apply the results of his experiments immediately and directly. This was all that he was interested in—solving practical problems to help humanity. He was not interested in research that could not be applied to help his fellow men. He would have scorned the idea of "science for science's sake," which is sometimes put forward by people who really have no idea what science is all about.

History is endlessly fascinating. For centuries, historians and philosophers have argued about how important is the individual person in shaping events, and how much he is dependent on his circumstances and his time. If Pasteur had lived in the fifteenth century, would he have achieved the same accomplishments? Perhaps not—though it is hard to imagine that such a man as Pasteur would not have made his mark whenever or wherever he had lived. The fact is, however, that Pasteur did live at the right time, and we are all enormously the better for his achievements.

But it was not enough for Pasteur to be a great scientist. In order for him to get his discoveries across to his colleagues, to convince the world, he had to be a great human being. He had to have a great store of integrity, courage, and perseverance.

The way in which he overcame a most serious illness, paralysis of half of his body, is a supreme example of his courage. No one could have blamed Pasteur

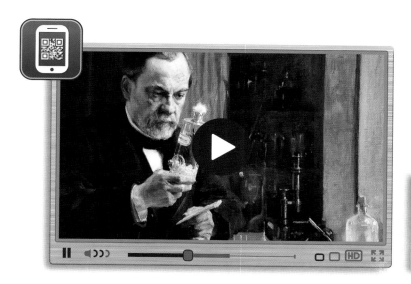

Scan here for a short video on the legacy of Louis Pasteur:

if he had just worked part-time when he recovered from paralysis. But at the earliest possible moment, he resumed working as hard as ever, and he continued to do so for the rest of his life.

With this great strength of character, one might have expected Pasteur to be a rigid and difficult person. Yet those who knew him testified to his excellence as a human being on a personal level. He was kindly, generous, and considerate to his family and his colleagues. His family life was a model of respectability and worthiness. He was tireless in doing all he could to help ordinary people anywhere. He was passionate and excitable—but only in the best of causes.

No one is perfect. Yet it is as foolish to be blind to human excellence as it is to see it everywhere. In the person of Louis Pasteur we can see a mixture of good qualities such as have rarely been found in the entire history of our race. And he lived just at the time and place when it was possible for his work and his example to bear fruit.

TEXT-DEPENDENT QUESTIONS

1. What disease did Pasteur's assistant at the Pasteur Institute seek to prevent?
2. Who was with Pasteur when he died in 1895?
3. What is Louis Pasteur's legacy?

 ## RESEARCH PROJECT

Using your school library or the internet, find out about the seventeenth century Italian scientist Franceso Redi, who conducted an experiment to refute the theory of spontaneous generation nearly 200 years before Pasteur. Write a short paper about Redi's experiment. What did he discover? How did his method of experimenting compare to Pasteur's method? Why were the conclusions he came to not accepted until Pasteur's time? Share your findings with your class.

Chronology

1822

Louis Pasteur is born at Dôle on December 27.

1827

Pasteur family moves to Arbois.

1838

Louis makes first visit to Paris.

1839–42

Secondary education at the Royal College at Besançon.

1842

Admitted to Ecole Normale Supérieure in Paris.

1842–43

Studies at the Lycée Saint-Louis, at the Sorbonne, and at the Institut Barbet in Paris.

1843

Readmitted to the Ecole Normale.

1844

Begins chemical and crystallographic studies. Discovers molecular asymmetry.

1846

Appointed assistant at Ecole Normale.

1847

Qualified as Doctor of Science.

1848
Appointed Professor of Chemistry at University of Strasbourg.

1848
Marriage to Marie Laurent on May 29.

1850
Birth of daughter Jeanne.

1851
Birth of son Jean-Baptiste.

1853
Birth of daughter Cécile. Awarded Legion of Honour for chemical studies.

1854
Appointed Professor of Chemistry in the faculty of Sciences at Lille University.

1855
Beginning of studies on fermentation.

1857
Appointed director of scientific studies at Ecole Normale Supérieure in Paris.

1858
Birth of daughter Marie-Louise.

1859
Death of daughter Jeanne. Begins studies on spontaneous generation.

1861
Discovery of anaerobic life.

1862
Elected to Academy of Sciences. Undertakes studies on acetic acid fermentation.

1863

Begins studies on wine. Appointed Professor of Geology, Physics and Chemistry at Ecole des Beaux Arts. Birth of daughter Camille.

1864

Publication of *Mémoire sur la fermentation acétique*. Controversy erupts over theory of spontaneous generation. Establishment of field laboratory at Arbois to study wine disease.

1865

Studies on pasteurization. Death of father and of youngest daughter, Camille.

1865–9

Begins to study silkworm diseases.

1866

Publication of essay on scientific achievements of Claude Bernard. Death of daughter Cécile.

1867

Receives Grand Prix of the Universal Exhibition for method of preservation of wines by heating. Appointed Professor of Chemistry at the Sorbonne.

1868

Publication of *Studies on Vinegar*. Attack of left-sided paralysis in October.

1869

Resumes study of silkworm diseases. Convalescence at Villa Vicentina.

1870

Returns to Paris. Franco-Prussian War begins.

1871

Searches for, and finds, his son. Returns to work in Paris at Ecole Normale.

The College de Sorbonne is a famous university in Paris where, as a student, Pasteur attended lectures by the famous chemist Jean-Baptiste Dumas. Pasteur later served as Professor of Chemistry at the Sorbonne in 1867.

1873

Elected associate member of the Academy of Medicine.

1876

Candidate for election to Senate but defeated. Publication of *Studies on Beer*.

1877

Begins studies of anthrax.

1878

Conducts studies on gangrene, septicemia, and childbirth fever.

1879
Begins studies on chicken cholera. Discovery of immunization by means of attenuated cultures. Marriage of daughter Marie-Louise to René Vallery-Radot. Marriage of son Jean-Baptiste.

1880
Begins to study rabies.

1881
Field trial of anthrax vaccine is successful.

1882
Election to Academy of Sciences.

1883
Vaccination against swine erysipelas developed. Conducts studies on cholera.

1885
Treatment of Joseph Meister against rabies is successful.

1886
International subscription held for foundation of Pasteur Institute.

1888
Inauguration of Pasteur Institute.

1892
Celebration of seventieth birthday at the Sorbonne.

1895
Dies on September 28.

Further Reading

Debré, Patrice. *Louis Pasteur*. Trans. by Elborg Forster. Baltimore: The Johns Hopkins Press, 2000.

Hunter, Nick. *Louis Pasteur*. Chicago: Raintree, 2014.

Jong-Kang Liu and King-Thom Chung. *Pioneers in Microbiology: The Human Side of Science*. Hackensack, N.J.: World Scientific, 2018.

Lassieur, Allison. *Louis Pasteur: Revolutionary Scientist*. New York: Scholastic, 2005.

Morus, Iwan Rhys. *The Oxford Illustrated History of Science*. New York: Oxford University Press, 2017.

Smith, Linda Wasmer. *Louis Pasteur: Genius Disease Fighter*. Berkeley Heights, N.J.: Enslow, 2015.

Waldman, Meredith. *The Vaccine Race; Science, Politics, and the Human Cost of Defeating Disease*. New York: Viking, 2017.

Wootton, David. *The Invention of Science: A New History of the Scientific Revolution*. New York: Harper Perennial, 2016.

Zamosky, Lisa. *Louis Pasteur and the Fight Against Germs*. Huntington Beach, Calif.: Teacher Created Materials, 2008.

Internet Resources

https://www.pasteur.fr/en

Website of the Pasteur Institute, an internationally renowned center for biomedical research. Its mission is to help prevent and treat diseases, mainly those of infectious origin, through research, teaching, and public health initiatives.

http://www.bbc.co.uk/timelines/z9kj2hv

The British Broadcasting Company (BBC) provides a short biography of Louis Pasteur at this site.

https://www.asm.org

The American Society for Microbiology is the world's oldest and largest life science organization. The official ASM website contains links to articles and exhibits related to microbiology.

http://www.pbs.org/wgbh/nova

The website of NOVA, a science series that airs on PBS. The series produces in-depth science programming on a variety of topics, from the latest breakthroughs in technology to the deepest mysteries of the natural world.

http://www.livescience.com

The website Live Science is regularly updated with articles on scientific topics and new developments or discoveries.

Series Glossary of Key Terms

anomaly—something that differs from the expectations generated by an established scientific idea. Anomalous observations may inspire scientists to reconsider, modify, or come up with alternatives to an accepted theory or hypothesis.

evidence—test results and/or observations that may either help support or help refute a scientific idea. In general, raw data are considered evidence only once they have been interpreted in a way that reflects on the accuracy of a scientific idea.

experiment—a scientific test that involves manipulating some factor or factors in a system in order to see how those changes affect the outcome or behavior of the system.

hypothesis—a proposed explanation for a fairly narrow set of phenomena, usually based on prior experience, scientific background knowledge, preliminary observations, and logic.

natural world—all the components of the physical universe, as well as the natural forces at work on those things.

objective—to consider and represent facts without being influenced by biases, opinions, or emotions. Scientists strive to be objective, not subjective, in their reasoning about scientific issues.

observe—to note, record, or attend to a result, occurrence, or phenomenon.

science—knowledge of the natural world, as well as the process through which that knowledge is built through testing ideas with evidence gathered from the natural world.

subjective—referring to something that is influenced by biases, opinions, and/or emotions. Scientists strive to be objective, not subjective, in their reasoning about scientific issues.

test—an observation or experiment that could provide evidence regarding the accuracy of a scientific idea. Testing involves figuring out what one would expect to observe if an idea were correct and comparing that expectation to what one actually observes.

theory—a broad, natural explanation for a wide range of phenomena in science. Theories are concise, coherent, systematic, predictive, and broadly applicable, often integrating and generalizing many hypotheses. Theories accepted by the scientific community are generally strongly supported by many different lines of evidence. However, theories may be modified or overturned as new evidence is discovered.

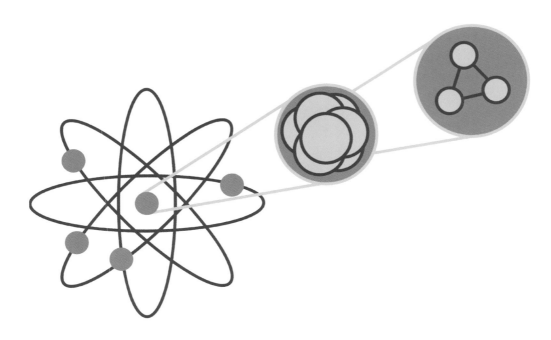

Index

About the Author

Harvey Warren received his undergraduate degree in history from the University of California at Berkeley, followed by graduate studies at the University of Pennsylvania. He has taught history, as well as Latin and Greek. Mr. Warren resides in Rancho Santa Fe, California, and lectures throughout the San Diego area.

Photo Credits

Centers for Disease Control: 62, 63; The Mutter Museum, Philadelphia: 13; used under license from Shutterstock, Inc.: 8, 10, 28, 42, 46, 87; Wellcome Library: 1, 6, 9, 11, 16, 19, 21, 22, 24, 25, 31, 33, 37, 38, 40, 48, 49, 50, 52, 55, 58, 67, 70, 72, 76, 78, 79, 80; Wikimedia Commons: 32, 39, 60, 73.